DO MORE
WITH
GOOGLE
CLASSROOM

Teach better.
Save time.
Make a difference.

MATT MILLER

Special discounts are available on quantity purchases by schools, school districts, associations, and others. Email books@daveburgessconsulting.com for pricing and details.

Published by Ditch That Textbook, an imprint of Dave Burgess Consulting, Inc.

DitchThatTextbook.com
DaveBurgessConsulting.com

Cover design by Najdan Mancic, Iskon Design Inc.
Interior design by Matt Miller

Library of Congress Control Number: 2020950762
Paperback ISBN: 978-1-951600-70-9
Ebook ISBN: 978-1-951600-71-6
First printing: December 2020

GoogleClassroomBook.com

For the brave teachers who made
the emergency adjustment to remote learning
during the COVID-19 pandemic in 2020.

Thank you for your tireless work
for the sake of your students.

CONTENTS

ACKNOWLEDGMENTS

'm grateful to my family, who continue to be my strongest supporters. My wife, Melanie, encourages me when my self-doubt tries to talk me out of doing something worthwhile. She gives me the perspective of a loving wife and a dedicated classroom teacher. My children — Cassie, Hallie, and Joel — remind me daily of the important work we do in education to grow our next generation of leaders. My parents, Jeff and Jacki, have unceasingly supported me. They've watched presentations, brainstormed in strategy sessions, and have even worked behind the scenes for me. I feel like I have the most supportive family ever. They've made possible anything I've endeavored to do in my professional life. I'm thankful for Karly Moura, my blog and social media editor. Her hard work and generous spirit to help educators has helped us to do what I could never do by myself. Her husband, John, and son, Jake, unselfishly support her work for Ditch That Textbook, and I'm truly grateful for that. Finally, and most importantly, I'm thankful to God, the author of my faith and the source of blessings and any success I've seen in my life.

For we are God's handiwork, created in Christ Jesus to do good works, which God prepared in advance for us to do.
— Ephesians 2:10 (NIV)

CRAFT THE CLASSROOM YOU WANT

During the COVID-19 pandemic of 2020, schools closed their doors to protect students and staff in a global pandemic. Students and teachers, sometimes overnight, were forced into emergency remote learning. Many teachers had little or no training on Google Classroom or many of the tech tools used for learning online.

It was kind of like the entrepreneurship parable of "building the plane while you're falling." Teachers tried to learn the tech as they gave assignments, all while trying to understand how remote learning was different than face-to-face learning.

The result: Anger. Confusion. Added stress to countless students and families who were already concerned about surviving the biggest pandemic in a century. It was time to bring the opposition down.

So, the students retaliated. In a sort of grassroots activism, they took to social networks like TikTok and Snapchat. They encouraged Google Classroom users to flood Apple's App Store with poor one-star ratings for Google Classroom. The app's overall rating plummeted to less than two stars on a five-star scale in short order.

After reading the reviews, it's clear that lots of the one-star reviewers use the word "glitchy." They describe bugs, like completed work marked as missing or the app crashing.

But if you read closely, there's more. You'll see children, parents and families crying out about stress, frustration and confusion of remote learning. In some cases, they're scared. They're hurt. Students, and even some parents, thought lashing out against the Google Classroom app might get the app canceled. And that might make the remote learning stop.

"Students are already stressed enough in these hard times of isolation," one student reviewer wrote. "It is only deteriorating our well-being and destroying our motivation to do any work. . . . If we continue using this application it will only have a negative effect on all students' mental health."

Another student: "I am already stressing about corona, and making sure I don't get sick and die, but now I have to worry about so much more, along with my grade suffering, and that's a lot to think about just for a teen like myself."

Criticisms can be made about learning online, from the lack of access to the lack of training to the lack of equity to marginalized groups. But that's a conversation for a different book.

What was at the heart of all those one-star reviews? Could the teachers have done anything differently? Sure, the app leaves some things to be desired. But an overall 1.5 stars out of five? It's something more than purported glitches and bugs in the app.

There's a lesson here we can use to improve our professional practice.

The one-star reviews weren't about Google Classroom.

Many were about how we, as teachers, were using Google Classroom.

It's not about the *app*.

It's about how we *use* the app.

(Note: It's entirely unfair to pin the blame on teachers, even though some people like to do that. The truth was that many teachers were forced to continue teaching remotely. Whether they were ready or trained to act, they were called to act. So, they acted. As we look at where the one-star backlash came from, it's not to criticize teachers who were poorly equipped to teach remotely.)

Google Classroom is a tool

Google Classroom is an assignment management tool. It was developed to create assignments, collect assignments, provide feedback and grades, and return assignments.

Whether you use the web browser version or a mobile app, Google Classroom has its limitations. It's not a full learning management system (LMS). Google Classroom is light and nimble. But what it does — manage assignments — it does pretty well.

When I defined Google Classroom as "an assignment management tool," note the word "tool." It's a tool. It's just a tool we use in our work to reach a desired outcome, just like a woodworker uses tools to craft something out of wood.

A woodworker sets out to build a beautiful chair out of wood. She collects the tools she'll need: hammer, drill, saw, etc. The tool doesn't determine what she is going to create. She doesn't search for a "chair-making saw." She doesn't cruise Amazon for a copy of *Chair Making with Saws for Dummies.* Creation goes far beyond the tool.

She starts, instead, with a dream of the chair she wants to make. She thinks about why she wants to make the chair. Where she'll put it in her home. The shape, curves and color to make it look just right.

She creates some plans, starting from the vision she has of the end product. She buys her materials: lumber, screws, wood glue, stain and varnish. Then, she starts creating.

Google Classroom is the teacher's

Chances are she will need to adjust her plans as she goes. (If her woodworking skills are anything like mine, it's a certainty she will adjust her plans!) But the goal isn't to have flawless, easy plans from the start. The goal is a beautiful chair. She may have to disassemble all of her work and start again to reach her goal. She may have to return to the home improvement store for more wood.

But when she's finished, she sees the fruits of her labor: the chair. It may be expertly crafted, exactly as she envisioned. The chair may fall short of her expectations. But in the end, it is *her* chair. She made it with her own two hands. She has a story to tell about that chair. And once she's finished, she is a better woodworker because of the lessons she learned while making it.

Google Classroom is the teacher's saw.

The teacher gets to use Google Classroom to help create the product she envisions. But it must start with a vision.

YouTube is full of Google Classroom product demos. Books and blog posts and support pages have been created to show you how to use Google Classroom step by step.

What many of them are missing, though, is the end product. The dream. The chair and the craftsmanship. How will students have learned? What is the transformation they will undergo? What will they have created? And how will they feel because of it?

This is a craftsmanship book. Sure, we will touch on some basics and how-to's. But the main goal is craft. This book addresses:

Not "how to make an assignment."
How to make a better assignment.

Not "how to arrange classwork."
How to arrange classwork effectively.

Not "how to quiz students."
How to truly assess what they know.

When you move from "how Google Classroom works" to "how to teach effectively with Google Classroom," you're making the most of teaching and learning with Classroom.

Do More with Google Classroom. Are you ready?

Note: Instructions and screenshots from Google Classroom were taken in 2020. Software changes frequently. Google Classroom's user interface may look different when you read this book. New features likely will have been added, and some features may have been removed. The solid teaching foundation this book is built upon, however, doesn't change and will remain throughout most changes. To find the most up-to-date changes in Google Classroom, visit the "What's new in Classroom" page in the Google Help Center at gclass.link/updates.

2

IMAGINE YOUR IDEAL CLASSROOM

The school year is about to start, and everything is fresh and new. New rosters of students. Those smiling faces will show up in your classroom soon enough. (Hey, it's the beginning of the year. We can still be optimistic for a few more days, right?)

New dry erase markers. (Let's be honest. Part of why we became teachers was for the school supplies.)

New, clean lesson plan book. (If you still use one of those, of course. I'm still all about a paper lesson plan book you can write in!)

When you open Google Classroom, your Classes page is empty and clean and ready to go — if you've archived all of your classes already.

Where do you start? What do you do? And how do you make sure your first moves are setting you up for success?

Imagine your ideal Classroom

Marie Kondo is the tidying guru. Her book, *The Life-Changing Magic of Tidying Up*, is a *New York Times* bestseller. She was named one of *Time* magazine's 100 Most Influential People in the World, and people worldwide have watched her Netflix show, *Tidying Up with Marie Kondo.*

If you've heard someone ask, "Does this spark joy?", it's because of Marie Kondo.

One of Marie's rules of tidying is "imagine your ideal lifestyle." It's the idea that you can't know where you're going until you have a vision and a plan.

> "When you imagine your ideal lifestyle, you are really clarifying why you want to tidy and **envisioning your best life**. The tidying process represents a turning point — so seriously consider **the ideal lifestyle to which you aspire.**"
>
> — Marie Kondo
> (KonMarie Media, Inc., 2020)

Have you ever considered your ideal Google Classroom lifestyle?Do you know what your best Google Classroom life looks like? "Come on, Matt," you may be thinking. "I'm just trying to figure out how to assign and grade my students' work. I'm not looking for an existential crisis right now."

Hey, I get you. We don't need to get too philosophical here. But it's hard to chart a course to a destination you haven't picked yet. If we try to set up your Google Classroom without knowing what's important to you, it's like walking through an unfamiliar house in the dark. You're bound to bang your shin on a table or fall down some stairs.

Ask yourself some of the questions on the next page. Continue to reflect on your ideal lifestyle for your teaching, for your students, for your classroom. Think about those and keep them in mind throughout this book. They'll help you make decisions and set up your Google Classroom — and your class — for success!

Be smart when you start

Making some smart moves at the beginning of the year can save you heartache. Plus, it can help your Google Classroom run smoothly all year. Thankfully, many of these smart moves can be made in the middle of the year, too. If you find your Google Classroom has turned into a hot mess, these can help you regain your sanity!

Smart start #1: Break up classes methodically

It would make sense to say that each class you teach gets a class in Google Classroom. But it's a little more complicated than that.

What if you have multiple sections of the same class?

What if you teach the same students all day? Do you just have one class?

What if your classes get too full of assignments after a semester (or a grading period)?

Envisioning your ideal Google Classroom

What goes in my **mission statement**? What's important to me as a teacher?

How do I prefer to **interact** with my students? What do they appreciate and value about our interactions?

What kind of **academic work** do I want my students to do: writing, speaking, recording, artistic work, etc.?

What are my personal preferences for **organizing**? In folders, with labels, with colors, etc.?

What do I value in **grading**? What kind of messages do I hope to send students with the grading process?

What **device** do I use most (or think I'll use most) to do schoolwork?

What if a project or assignment type takes up lots of space in a class? Do you spawn a new class just for that?

How you break up classes in Google Classroom is one of the first organizational decisions you make in a school year. The bad news: *It's a decision that's hard to change if you don't get it right.* The good news*: It's not a deal breaker, and you can do it differently next time.*

Some teachers will create new Google Classroom classes every semester — or grading period — to keep a class from getting too full. Some elementary teachers will create different classes for each subject they teach (reading, math, science, etc.). Some will create classes for special projects or assignment types (like weekly writing assignments).

To create your own strategy, think about the key distinctions of your classes. What makes them different? What do you do a lot of? What's important? These can help guide your decisions.

Smart start #2: Name your classes carefully

Create a class by clicking on the plus button (+) on the Classes page of Google Classroom. When you do, it prompts you to provide a class name, a section, a subject and a room.

From an organizational standpoint, two of these are more important than the others: *class name* and *section*. These two are displayed everywhere: in the menu sidebar, on tiles on the Classes page, at the top of an active classroom, and in the classroom header. You can only find *subject* and *room* by clicking the dropdown icon in the classroom header.

You can pick whatever you want to go in the name and section fields. They have two important jobs. One: students must distinguish between their classes. They need to be able to scan their classes and find the one they need. Two: *you* must distinguish between *your* classes. You need to identify the class you're looking for quickly and without confusion. For both, the quicker, the better.

If quick identification is your goal in naming your class, then don't overdo it. Be brief: short and clear.

Also, emojis can help! You can add emojis (also called emoticons) to your class name, section, subject, and room. A unique emoji at the beginning of the name of each class can help accomplish both naming goals. Each emoji, if different, helps you distinguish between classes at a quick glance. It does the same for students — especially if their other teachers aren't using emojis!

Smart start #3: Make your banner work for you

Certain parts of Google Classroom are very visible to your students. These parts are often at the top of the page or in a place where students often look. I call these places "prime real estate." They're in an important, helpful spot. We should make the most of our prime real estate and make it work for us!

The class banner in Google Classroom is prime real estate. Your class banner is the image that displays at the top of your class in Google Classroom and in the tile in the Classes section. Students are likely to see your class banner every time they access your class.

Your class is assigned a banner when it's created, and it's easy to change. When you open your class, you can click two options on your banner image: *select theme* and *upload photo*. It's easy to click **Select theme** and choose an existing banner image.

But your banner can work harder than that for you. It's prime real estate, remember?

By adding your own banner image to your class, you can:

- Display photos of your class and individual students
- Share announcements and news about your students
- Provide answers to common questions
- Display your class slogan, mission statement, or norms
- Provide reminders about deadlines and important upcoming dates

You can create a banner image very simply. Open a new Google Slides or Google Drawings file. Go to **File > Page setup** and customize the dimensions to 1,600 pixels by 400 pixels.

When you design your banner, remember that the class name, the class code, the Meet link and the links to edit the banner are placed on the banner image. You might avoid placing anything in those areas. Also, when your banner displays on a tile in your Classes section, it cuts off roughly a quarter of the banner on the right side.

When you're done, go to **File > Download as > PNG image**. Then, in your Google Classroom class, click **Upload photo** on the banner and upload your new image. Download a template that can help you make a banner at gclass.link/banner.

The more you update your banner, the more students will look for the changes. If they create the habit of looking for new Google Classroom banner images, this can be a great place to keep students up to date and build classroom community.

Smart start #4: Set up posting on the Stream

Your Stream in Google Classroom is like the social media feed for your class. You and your students can see new posts there with the most recent at the top. When something new happens, it shows up at the top of the stream. (By the way, you can bump a post to the top of your stream by clicking the three dots menu button and choosing **Move to top**.)

It's up to you to determine how social this social media feed gets in your classroom. You can choose whether students can post to the stream and whether they can comment. You can find this in the settings gear button under Stream.

The option that you choose for students — post and comment, comment only, or none — should match your goals for the class. Is there a reason that students would post on their own? Do you want them to post to encourage each other? To share something that's important to them? Do you want to encourage a discussion forum where students have some control?

Ah, that word. *Control*. Some of our decisions on this setting relate to control. Are we willing to release some of our control? Can we live with the uncertainty of what students may post if we turn over some of the control? Much of this decision has to do with intention, too. Giving students free reign on posts and comments doesn't make you a good teacher by itself. Creating the environment where students can express themselves and feel a sense of ownership is powerful. But you also don't want to force an environment where students post that isn't authentic and natural to the learning setting. Your decision here should be intentional.

You might consider setting some norms on posting and/or commenting that aren't overly loose or restrictive. Help students to see what the goal of the posts and comments is. Help them to see what it looks like when it's done well. Also, consider giving students input on what those norms may look like and how to use this feature. They may have experienced an uncomfortable online forum through social media at some point. If they don't want to experience it again, they may have ideas on how to set it up effectively. And let's be honest. They may have more experience than the teacher!

More tips to set up for success

Here are some other tips and strategies for setting up your Google Classroom well from the beginning:

Drag your tiles. On the Classes page, you can drag the tiles for all of your classes into any order that you choose. You might put them in chronological order. Or you might use a more fluid organization, like dragging the classes you need to assign or grade next to the top.

Get your students set up. After you've set up your classes, one of the easiest tasks is enrolling students in them. Students can log in to Google Classroom and click the plus button (+) to join a class. Display the class code by clicking it in the banner at the top of your class. You can also provide students with a join link. Copy it by clicking the class code in the banner and choosing **Copy invite link**. You can email it or provide it somewhere that's accessed easily by students.

Turn on guardian emails. This is a quick, no-prep solution to keep parents and guardians in the loop on what's going on in class. In your class settings, you can turn on guardian emails. Invite guardians by clicking the People tab in your class and choosing **Invite guardians** next to the students' names. Your school district Google admin can add guardian emails in bulk, too, so it may already be done for you. These emails are automatically sent to guardians, which is an extra incentive to keep your Google Classroom up to date. *It may send a summary to guardians with something you haven't updated yet,* so be aware of that before you turn it on!

Need some help with the basics?

Check out the Google Classroom Quick-Start Guide with lots of tutorials, step-by-step guides, and tips for learning Google Classroom 101. It also includes a FREE downloadable ebook! Go to gclass.link/quick to get started.

3

GET AND STAY ORGANIZED

Want to know how cool I was in college? I definitely wasn't "big man on campus." Know how you could tell? I had a Palm Pilot. As a college freshman.

Know what I'm talking about? A Palm Pilot was a precursor to today's iPhone. It was a PDA: *personal digital assistant.* You could take notes with it. You could keep a calendar. There were even games you could download on it. You just couldn't make calls or send texts.

In my own mind, I was super cool. I took that Palm Pilot everywhere. I brought it to my college classes and took notes on it. I didn't have a keyboard, though. I used the stylus and a series of gestures to create each letter. It wasn't very fast or efficient, but it got the job done. I got scolded by one of my professors once for using it. "You know," he told me, "one of these days that thing is going to fail and you're going to be out of luck."

He was wrong. For me, that Palm Pilot saved time and made me way more efficient. The reason? I knew where everything was. I could find my appointments on my calendar. I kept to-do lists and checked items off. I didn't lose my notes because they were always on that device.

The reason the Palm Pilot worked for me was because I knew where everything was. For once, I was finally organized. The same principles apply to your Google Classroom. When you — and your students — know where to find everything you need, you don't even think about it anymore. Instead, you're thinking about the learning and the work. And that's exactly how teachers and students should spend their brain power.

In this chapter, we'll delve into some organizational strategies you can use in Classroom. Everyone benefits when your Google Classroom isn't a hot mess.

Topics: Your organizational superpower

The part of your Google Classroom that is easiest to fall into disarray is the Classwork page. You add assignments, quizzes, questions, and materials to this page. Unfortunately, if you don't have a strategy for keeping these organized, the Classwork page ends up like the junk drawer in your kitchen. It contains lots of stuff you want to keep. It's just next to impossible to find anything.

Thankfully, Google has made the Classwork page much easier to manage and navigate over time. One of the biggest game-changing inventions there was *topics*. Topics are headings you can add to the Classwork page. Use the **Create** button to add a new one.

Think of them like file folders in a filing cabinet. Put a label on the folder and stick it in the drawer. If you use it — and put files in those folders — your filing cabinet is neatly organized and easy to navigate.

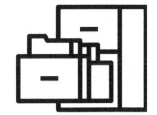

So, what do we put on those labels on our file folders? How do we organize our topics in our Classwork page?

Organizing topics on your Classwork page

There are lots of methods for arranging your topics. Some teachers will use one of these methods — or a derivative of these — without variation. Others will pick and choose and create a hybrid. Come up with something you think will work best for you and your students and try it. Thankfully, if it flops, it's easy to change topics and drag files around on your Classwork page.

- **By week:** Each week of the school year gets its own topic.
- **By unit:** Each unit or chapter in your curriculum gets its own topic.
- **By category:** Any category or subject that has classwork items gets its own topic.
- **By file type:** Assignments, quizzes, materials, and questions all get their own topic. (This one is not as effective for a regular classroom but could be helpful in some situations.)

A general rule of thumb for organizing your Classwork page is to arrange in reverse chronological order, with the most recent items at the top. The reason this works so well is because the

PRIME REAL ESTATE

top of the Classwork page is prime real estate! The top of the Classwork page is going to be seen by your students much more frequently than the bottom.

I majored in journalism in college and worked as a newspaper reporter before becoming a teacher. In journalism, they teach you to use a style of writing called the inverted pyramid. In this style, you put the most important news at the top. The first sentence or paragraph is called the lead. (For some reason, journalists spell it "lede.") Everything else that follows is ranked in order

MOST IMPORTANT

LEAST IMPORTANT

of importance. That way, if an editor needs to cut the story down to size, she can chop the bottom off and keep the most pertinent facts in the story.

The inverted pyramid works with your Classwork page, too. Let's put the most important items at the top, followed by progressively less important items. The older an assignment is, logically, the less important it is on a day-to-day basis.

Organize more deeply with subtopics

When I taught high school Spanish, organizing by unit made the most sense to me. My curriculum was organized into six main units. But each unit had three chapters, and each chapter had multiple lessons. Unit. Chapter. Lesson. That's three levels of organization! If I organized all of that with units as my main topics, I'd end up dividing a whole school year into just six unit topics on my Classwork page. Each topic would be too cluttered to be helpful!

Google Classroom can't create a hierarchy of topics and subtopics like a research paper outline. (At least it doesn't as of the publication of this book.) No matter what you teach, if you're like me, you want the ability to customize your organization strategy to suit your needs. Thankfully, you can create your own subtopics by being smart about how you name your topics.

Let's use my Spanish curriculum as an example. It has three levels of organization: units, chapters, and lessons. Because Google Classroom doesn't support creating a hierarchy like that, I'm going to make one myself in the way I type the title of my topics.

With this organization strategy, I label each unit as "U1," "U2," and so on. I label chapters as "Ch1," "Ch2," and I label lessons as "L1," "L2," etc. It's important to keep them in the same order and use the same abbreviations each time. Why? This makes your topics very scannable. Students can scroll up and down your Classwork page, fixing their eyes on the part of the page where the unit number passes by as they scroll up and down. Then, they watch the chapter number and then the lesson number until they find what they need. A little summary next to the abbreviations helps everyone remember what that particular lesson is about.

By using this strategy, you can create a hierarchy of topics and subtopics as simple or complex as you'd like!

Get to know this keyboard shortcut

Even if your Classwork page is organized tightly, it's going to get long. The more assignments you create, the harder it will be to find things — especially if they were assigned a while back. There are some strategies you can use when naming your assignments that can help (more on that later). If you use a simple keyboard shortcut, you can save yourself and your students a ton of time.

Ctrl+F

(It's Command+F on Mac computers.)

Ctrl+F is the *find* shortcut. It lets you search an entire webpage for a specific word or phrase. Many of us know it exists when asked about it, but sometimes we don't think to use it in the moment when it could be helpful.

If you make student training on **Ctrl+F** a part of your first days of school, it can save you and your students lots of time and headaches. This is a very practical skill they can use to scan webpages, documents, even transcripts of online videos to find exactly what they need. Teach them to use it on the Classwork page to find assignments, materials, quizzes, and questions.

One caveat: the Classwork page doesn't load all the classwork when the page loads. It loads *some* of it, and there's a **View more** button. For students to be able to use **Ctrl+F**, they'll need to click **View more** until the assignment loads. An easy, mindless way to handle this: just hit **View more** until all the assignments load, then use **Ctrl+F** to find the one they're looking for. Just search for a word that you know will be in the assignment title.

The Right Now topic

By organizing your Classwork page in reverse chronological order — or with the inverted pyramid — you'll have the most important items at the top of the page. (You remember that the top of the page is prime real estate, right?) This is helpful, but there's one more trick you can use to make the top of the page work even harder for you.

That trick is to create a Right Now topic at the top of the Classwork page. The content in the Right Now topic is constantly changing and fluid. It's where you put the items that you know your students will be looking for on that day — or even in that moment.

Creating a new assignment where they might need to review a material you posted earlier? Move both to the Right Now topic.

Reviewing some concepts from earlier in the month? Move them to the Right Now topic.

Working on one activity in the morning and another in the afternoon? Put the morning one in the Right Now topic. Then move it out at lunchtime and put the afternoon activity there.

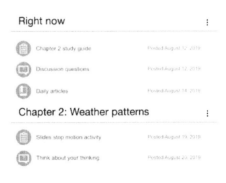

Your Classwork page is fluid. You can always move anything around at any time to better suit your needs and those of your students. Students will learn to expect lots of change to the Right

Now section. When the day or class period is over, you can file the items in your Right Now section back in the corresponding

Classwork page topic. (You're such a tidying guru!)

Think of the "right now" section like the workspace on your desk. Ideally, you don't store lots of things long-term on your desk. You grab what you need, work on it, then return it to the location that's best to store it. That's the idea behind your "right now" section.

Does it have to be called Right Now? Nope! It could be called Today or What You Need Now. You could have a Today section and a Yesterday section. You could have a Missing Work section under your Right Now section.

What you put at the top of your Classwork page shows **how you prioritize** and what you think students are **most likely to need**.

More Google Classroom tips to stay organized

There's more to staying organized with Google Classroom than using topics in your Classwork page. Here are some other ideas that might help.

Copy a link to a Google Classroom assignment. In the Classwork page, you can click the three dots button next to an assignment, quiz, question or material and choose **Copy link**. These links make it easy to get students to an assignment they need to finish. Just copy the link and email it to the student. You must be logged in as someone with access to the class the assignment is in to view the assignment. This means you can't email a link and have a parent view the assignment with his/her own Google account.

View student work in the class Drive folder. When students turn in work for an assignment, the work lives in a shared folder in Google Drive called "Google Classroom." In this folder are subfolders for your classes, and then sub-subfolders for assignments. These folders contain student work and are only for you. Students don't have access to them. Students have folders *like* these, but their folders contain only their own work. These folders can be an easy way to find work easily.

Move to top of Stream. The Stream is a list of activity from your class sorted in reverse chronological order. Whenever something is posted to Google Classroom, it shows up on the Stream. The top of the Stream is a high-visibility location. It's the first

PRIME REAL ESTATE

thing students see after they open your class. That means the top of the Stream is prime real estate! Want to make it work harder for you? Move something important to the top of the Stream. Click the three dots menu button for the item you want to move. Choose **Move to top** to bring it to the top of the list. (I mentioned this briefly in Chapter 2, also.)

You just made Google Classroom easier on everyone!

Great work on getting your Google Classroom organized! Whether they thank you on the outside, your students thank you on the inside. If they knew how much easier you made their experience in Classroom, they'd make you a cake. Or buy you flowers. Or bring you coffee. Or maybe all three!

OK. The foundation is in place. Your Google Classroom is set up and you have some organizational principles. Now it's time to create some assignments! You can take steps to improve your assignments — from good to great!

Google Classroom loves virtual learning

If you and your students have access to Google tools, it opens lots of options for remote learning. This works whether you're doing full-time virtual learning or are trying to provide extra options to students at home. For ideas on doing better remote learning with G Suite — including Google Meet — go to <u>gclass.link/remote</u>.

CREATE GREAT ASSIGNMENTS

Assignments are the engine that runs Google Classroom. It's pretty safe to say that the majority of what most teachers fill their Classwork pages up with are assignments.

It only makes sense. Assignments let you . . .

- Provide details for your assignments
- Attach important documents, files, and links
- Keep tabs on students as they work
- Collect their digital work when finished
- Grade and provide feedback without carrying papers around

Not all assignments are created equally, though. Some are better than others. You can take steps to level up your assignments in Google Classroom, making the most of its features.

Step 1: Think and plan first

Planning an assignment in Google Classroom is a lot like planning a traditional in-class assignment. But going from a traditional, face-to-face, no-tech class to a digital classroom isn't always a simple transition. Here are five things to keep in mind before you create a Google Classroom assignment:

Keep an eye on your goals

Before you create an assignment, it's a good idea to think about what your goals are for your students. Assignments are more than grades in a gradebook. Make sure that they're a means to an end — a way to help students reach goals for the day, week, unit, etc. When you make a Google Classroom assignment, it's a good idea to ask, "Is this assignment helping the students reach goals? Which goals? How will I know that they've reached them?"

Reverse curriculum design still applies

Start with the end in mind, right? What should students know, demonstrate, be able to do when they're done? Some teachers will plan or even build out their assessments for the end of a chapter or unit so they're clear on what they want students to accomplish. (More on Google Classroom assessments in a later chapter.)

Hook their hearts before you hook their minds

Student engagement is key, too. How are you going to hook your students into learning? How are you going to get them excited or curious? Excited *and* curious? Some examples:

- A funny image or video
- A provocative question
- A surprise
- A connection to students' lives
- A mystery to solve
- A story with conflict

Don't stop that important engagement work at the beginning of the lesson! Keep finding ways to draw students in. Teaching doesn't have to be like force-feeding raw vegetables. You can add some seasoning and still stay nutritious.

Traditional lessons don't always go digital easily

A common misconception is that you can just port any lesson you've taught in class over to Google Classroom. Turn paper to digital. Turn instruction (spoken) into instructions (written). Sometimes that works. But a traditional in-person lesson has its strengths and advantages. So does a digital assignment in Google Classroom. Make the most of the strengths. If you try to switch seamlessly between the two without any adjustment, sadly, your best lessons may be set up for disaster.

Tailor the lesson to the strengths of the platform

Google Classroom is a great place to store and organize resources. It's a great place to host work that students do together. It lends itself to immediate, collaborative feedback in many places. And that's just the beginning. When you realize what you like best about a teaching platform (and we can call face-to-face, in-person teaching a platform), you accentuate the positives.

Step 2: Give your assignment a title

In this book, we've touched on a few spots in Google Classroom that are prime real estate. These are high visibility spots that can work hard for us and our students.

The assignment title is one of those spots. These titles are prime real estate because they show up in lots of places: on the Classwork page, on the Stream, in the gradebook, in guardian email summaries, and more. Get them right and your Classroom will be crystal clear and working like clockwork. Otherwise, you'll have confused questions like, "Which assignment called 'Writing activity' was it? The first one, the second one, or the one in all caps?"

Here are some keys to making the most of this prime real estate:

Assignment titles should be descriptive

In a few words, a great title summarizes the entire activity in a way that sets it apart from others. It doesn't have to be as tricky as picking the perfect title for your autobiography. (You're going to write one of those, right? Because we want to read it!) It does depend on some key words and phrases. Include the most important words in your title — even if it doesn't make for a grammatically perfect phrase!

Assignment titles should be numbered

This one isn't mandatory, but I think it should be. Put a unique number on every Google Classroom assignment. I like beginning an assignment title with its number. I got this idea from education blogger and math teacher Alice Keeler (alicekeeler. com). It makes sense. At times, you'll need to talk to students about a particular assignment — when work is incomplete, when students are absent, etc. Identifying it by number saves you both time and confusion.

Assignment titles should be categorized

Warning: if color coding and categorizing excite you, this section will be like a fistful of colored highlighters! A quick and simple way to categorize is with emojis. Add the same specific emoji every time to titles for a certain type of assignment or topic. Students will know immediately what kind of assignment they're opening. Another way to categorize is to use topics. You organize an assignment, a quiz, a material or a question under a topic. There's a left sidebar for topics on the Classwork page to keep you organized.

Step 3: Write clear instructions

I've fallen victim to this one many times. Sometimes, in my classroom, I would create an assignment on the fly without instructions. It was fine for work done in class that day. But if I failed to write solid instructions, absent students suffered. Students who didn't finish work in class suffered. Students who didn't pay great attention to my verbal directions — or those who were unclear — suffered. (Note: Sometimes, we give students lots of verbal instructions in class. If they ask us later to repeat parts of them, it might not mean they weren't paying attention. A slew of verbal instructions is a lot to carry in your working memory — especially while doing academic work!)

Take the time to write out detailed instructions. Everyone benefits.

Here are some ways to improve your Google Classroom instructions — in assignments, quizzes, and questions.

Revise your instructions

Have you ever written instructions, hurriedly posted them, and read them later, wondering what you were thinking when you wrote them? This has happened to me a lot! It may seem obvious, but taking a moment to re-read your work helps. Also, having someone else read your instructions can help identify vague or unclear directions — especially someone who isn't a teacher or doesn't teach the same content you do.

When something changes in your assignment, try to remember to update the instructions in Classroom. This helps you — and students — avoid assignments that don't reflect the most recent changes. I've had this one backfire on me before, too.

Make your instructions easy to read

No one likes to read a huge block of text. It's hard on the eyes. Our brains like to look on a page for white space where our eyes can rest. This has become a common practice in online writing. Online articles, blog posts — really, anything with text — often include plenty of white space so they don't hurt our brains.

Break up your instructions with double returns. Don't just hit return once; hit it twice to create an extra line of space. And add bullet points. Classroom doesn't support bullets or rich text formatting (as of publication of this book). You can create them yourself by adding hyphens or other characters as bullets. Emojis make fun bullet points, and Classroom supports them!

Be concise. Often, saying it in 10 words is better than 18. Seven words is better than 12. Try to be concise as long as you're not cutting out valuable details. It's easy for students to get lost in a sea of words. When teachers complain that students don't read their instructions, sometimes it's because those instructions are too long!

Step 4: Provide attachments that are helpful

One of the most powerful features of Google Classroom is its integration with the tools in G Suite, like Docs, Slides, Sheets, Drawings, and more. Including the right attachments equips your students and can add an extra dimension to your lessons. Below are some of the types of attachments you can add to an assignment, quiz, material or question. In the coming chapters, you'll see some examples of how you can use them.

Add the right amount of attachments

It's super easy to add attachments to Google Classroom assignments. But we don't want them to become a dumping ground for lots of stuff your students realistically won't use. Don't add them because it feels like you should; add attachments because they serve a purpose.

Add "make a copy" attachments for individual work

If students need their own personal space to think through an assignment or reflect, making a copy is great. When you attach a file and choose **Make a copy**, it automatically distributes copies of that file to each student *and* adds the students' names to the file name.

Collaborate with "everyone can edit" attachments

Some of the best attachments may be files where you don't do much more than create a blank workspace. Create an empty collaborative space for students in a Doc or Slides. Then attach the file to the assignment and choose **Everyone can edit**. Watch a video on setting this up at gclass.link/shared. When you create collaborative spaces, be sure to think ahead about...

- How collaboration enhances the assignment
- What students should do in the space
- What behavior is appropriate for the space

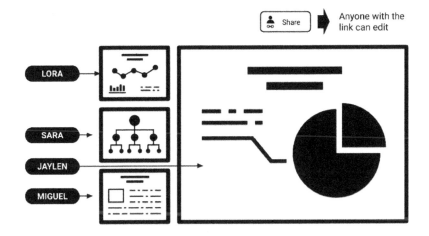

A word of caution about attachments

Attachments provide a very efficient way to distribute digital versions of mindless electronic worksheets. Resist the temptation to do that. Remember that classroom technology is an opportunity to teach differently, to improve what we do. When we use technology to teach the same way we did without it, we're squandering the gift — the opportunity to do something amazing. Keep asking yourself, "How could the technology make the learning experience better?"

Creating assignments is just the beginning!

After reading this chapter, you have some practical strategies to make the most of the assignments you create. Now comes the fun part! In the next chapter, we're going to take our assignments to the next level, stretching the limits of what you can do with assignments! If you've ever thought that Classroom seems a bit drab with assignments full of documents and slide presentations, you're in for a treat — with lots of practical examples you can use!

Get great Google Classroom resources

This book is just the beginning of the resources I've gathered for you on using Google Classroom. The companion website, GoogleClassroomBook.com, is full of blog posts, videos, tutorials, and templates you can copy and assign to your students. The ideas you find there are additional to what you'll find in this book. Check back to the website often as we add new material!

5

STRETCH ASSIGNMENTS TO THE LIMITS

When you look at Google Classroom the first time, it's easy to feel a bit, well, underwhelmed. It doesn't seem like there are many moving pieces. There's a Stream. There's a Classwork tab. There's a place for grades. There's not much else.

At first glance, it seems like Google Classroom doesn't do very much. You might think, "With all of the buzz around it, I expected Classroom have more bells and whistles!"

It *does* have lots of possibilities! The problem is that you might be looking in the wrong place.

Google Classroom is like an airport

Let's imagine that you're taking the spring break vacation of your dreams. (Or maybe you're more of a summer break vacationer.

You can go with that if you want.) You've been planning this trip for years and it's finally becoming a reality.

Google Classroom is like **an airport**, taking you to a wide world of **creative assignments.**

When you think of the trip, what's the first thing you see in your mind? Sandy beaches? Gorgeous views? A mountaintop cabin? You're probably not thinking about the airport, right?

An airport is not the destination of the vacation of your dreams. Google Classroom isn't the destination either. It's a means to an end. It's a way to get to a wide world of creative assignments your students can do.

The power of Google Classroom is that you can link students to all kinds of apps and sites to do their work. Let's call some of them "domestic flights." These exist within the confines of G

Suite, like Docs and Slides and Sheets. Others we'll call "international flights." They are outside of G Suite, like Flipgrid and Adobe Spark and Quizizz.

Students can show what they know by going to any of these destinations to create something. Then they can turn that creation in to you through Google Classroom. G Suite tools like Docs and Slides and Sheets are all integrated with Google Classroom. Students have the option of turning in a file from their Google Drive to Google Classroom. With other non-G Suite tools, students can download their work, then upload it to Google Drive and turn it in. Or they get a shareable link directly to their work in the other app.

With Google Classroom, you just have to know **what's possible** and **where you want to go**.

They can attach that to their Google Classroom assignment to turn in. Just ask the student to make sure they have given you access to their file when they turn it in.

You can see how Google Classroom is like an airport. It links out to all sorts of activities in different apps much like an airport connects you to destinations around the world. You go to the airport to get somewhere else. With Google Classroom, you go there to get somewhere else, too. It's the connection point your students use to learn. The quality of your vacation is based on the imagination and planning you use to get there. The airport is just the mechanism you use to get where you want to go. Similarly, Google Classroom will take you and your students to great destinations. You just have to know what's possible and where you want to go.

So, where will you go? What will you do?

Now that we know all about Google Classroom International Airport, it's time to purchase a ticket! You're standing at the ticket counter ready to purchase. (I'm told that people really used to buy airline tickets this way. You know, before the internet was a thing.)

You check out the departures board to see where flights are going today. This is your big moment. You're not going just anywhere. It's got to be a destination that makes your heart sing.

Here are some departing flights — digital tools that can take your Google Classroom assignments to new heights.

1. Create a top 5 video in Flipgrid.

What is Flipgrid? Flipgrid is a free video response tool. The teacher creates a topic (a question or a prompt). Students respond by recording short video clips. If you want, you can set it up so students can watch each other's videos and respond to them.

What's a top 5 video? You're likely to find top 10 videos all over YouTube. When YouTubers create videos like these, they appeal to viewers for several reasons. One reason is that the video is a list. YouTube viewers like to know that they'll see lots of examples in these videos. Another reason is that the video creator ranks the items in the videos. They tell us what's best, and we compare where our favorites rank. We can agree or disagree with the rankings.

These videos are super easy to create on Flipgrid, and they can be a great academic task. I like to alter them to top 5 videos in many cases because 10 examples end up being a lot for an assignment. But if a top 10 works for what you're doing, then go with it!

Create a Flipgrid topic for your students for the assignment. Describe what you want students to do (e.g. why you put it in your top 5, why it deserves that ranking, what you didn't include in the list). Provide a link to the assignment for students in Google Classroom (or just use the **Share to Google Classroom** link).

When students record, I'd encourage them to add text to their videos to summarize the topic and talk about each selection on the list. They can add text boxes to their videos to create a title and list each item as they talk about it. I'd also encourage them to pause the video to change the text (and anything else on the screen, like images or other effects) between each selection. When they're done, their videos are automatically uploaded to the Flipgrid topic where you can see them. (Other students can see them, too, if you've set it up that way.)

For a step-by-step guide to making top 5 videos — with tips and different versions your students can try — go to gclass.link/top5.

2. Create a Yelp-style review in Google Slides.

What is Google Slides? You probably know that it's a slide presentation tool (like PowerPoint). But it can be used for much, much more than just slides for oral presentations in class. I love how easy it is to do graphic design on Google Slides, and that graphic design lets us create all sorts of creative learning experiences for students.

What is a Yelp-style review? Consumers review restaurants, coffee shops, plumbers, hotels and more on Yelp. They rate businesses with a five-star scale. They can include a description and photos from their experience. Writing a review like those found on Yelp can be a valuable and fun academic task. In its most basic form, a Yelp-style review can help students form opinions, justify them, and back them up with evidence. Students can go even deeper, writing a review from the perspective of a character in a book, a historical character, or someone in pop culture or current news.

Do students need the Yelp app to complete this activity? Do they need to create a Yelp account? Thankfully, no! This is one of the key ideas in my book *Tech Like a PIRATE*, which is all about fun, memorable learning experiences with tech. You don't need the app to create the experience. We can recreate the experience of using Yelp with an app that students can access: Google Slides. (This also works with PowerPoint. But if you're reading this book about Google Classroom, I'm betting that your students are more likely to use Google Slides.)

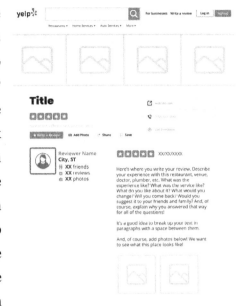

I've created a Google Slides Yelp file you can copy and assign to your students through Google Classroom. Go to gclass.link/yelp and copy it into your Google Drive. Then, when you create an assignment in Google Classroom, attach that Google Slides Yelp file to your assignment. Be sure to click the three dots button on the attachment and select **Make a copy for each student**.

Students open their own copy of the file. They can change the title, type of business, contact information, date of review, person writing the review, and more. They can add images to the review and choose the number of stars. When they finish, they can turn it in to you through Google Classroom. You can find more Google Slides templates like this at gclass.link/templates.

DESTINATION
SCREENCASTIFY
FLIGHT TYPE
INTERNATIONAL
ITINERARY
CREATE AN
EXPLAINER VIDEO.

SEAT
24C

BOARDING ZONE
D3

GATE
A8

BOARDING ZONE
D3

DEPARTURE
3:15

SEAT
24C

✈ CLASSROOM AIRLINES

3. Create an explainer video with Screencastify.

What is Screencastify? Screencastify is a screen recording tool. It's an extension you can install in your Google Chrome web browser. (Find instructions at screencastify.com.) With it, you can record video of your screen, of your webcam, or a combination of both. You can also record audio narration with your microphone throughout your video. When you're finished recording, you can do some simple video editing. The video is automatically uploaded to Google Drive, which makes it easy to turn screen recording videos in as assignments. Screencastify offers paid features, but its free plan is pretty feature-packed. Other tools like Loom and Awesome Screenshot will let you record your screen for free, too.

What is an explainer video? An explainer video is simply a video that explains something, ideally in an easy-to-understand way. It's created to simplify life for the viewer in some way. Screencast videos are great for this. Some concepts are just easier to demonstrate on a computer screen than others.

You can create slides with Google Slides and record a video showing the slides and talking about them.

When students record their voices to describe thinking, it's almost like we can **peer inside their minds.**

Or you can draw on a digital whiteboard and record your screen while you draw. Find several online whiteboard apps at gclass.link/whiteboard.

You can even put several images, shapes, text boxes, and more on a slide in Google Slides. While in edit mode (i.e. don't push **Present**), record your screen as you drag them around the screen to sort them or make sense of them.

You can record an online map to give a virtual tour of sorts. Google Maps Street View and Google Earth make for great virtual walking tour activities when you record yourself with a screen recording tool. Learn how to do this at gclass.link/tour.

Students can create these videos with Screencastify in Google Chrome. When done, the videos can be uploaded automatically to Google Drive. Students can turn these videos in by attaching the video in Google Drive to the assignment in Google Classroom.

The most powerful part of this activity is hearing the students describe their thinking. When they record their voices as they talk through their thought process, it's almost like we can peer inside their minds, giving us more insight.

Other destinations for Google Classroom assignments

You've seen three destinations you can travel to from Google Classroom International Airport: Flipgrid, Google Slides and Screencastify. You and your students can use lots of other tools in a variety of ways, and Google Classroom can be the jumping-off point.

Beware of adding too many destinations to your airport, though! When students have to bounce from digital tool to digital tool too often, it can get very frustrating. In each new tool, there are new buttons and features. There's a new user interface to get used to. Sometimes, there are new usernames and passwords for different tools. All that switching can be a headache for students. The longer it takes to learn a new tool, the less time is spent on task. Consider focusing your efforts on a few tools that work in a variety of ways for you and your students. When you vary your approach to one tool, your students can enjoy variety and change without having to learn how to use something new.

How to find more destinations

Assignments in Google Classroom are only limited to the destinations you know about — that is, the digital tools you can use in conjunction with Classroom. To broaden your horizons, you can find more tools or find more uses for them.

Where can you find new tools — and creative ways to use them? Here are some of my favorites:

Follow educator blogs, websites, and podcasts. These are sources created by educators for educators where they share what's working for them. Read blogs for how-to articles and lists of ideas. Listen to podcasts during your commute or on your downtime.

DOMESTIC FLIGHTS

Tools inside G Suite

Jamboard
jamboard.google.com

Drawings
drawings.google.com

Docs
docs.google.com

Forms
forms.google.com

INTERNATIONAL FLIGHTS

Tools not included in G Suite

Adobe Spark
spark.adobe.com

Edpuzzle
edpuzzle.com

Quizlet
quizlet.com

Book Creator
bookcreator.com

Quizizz
quizizz.com

Synth
gosynth.com

Kahoot!
kahoot.com

Flipgrid
flipgrid.com

Register for the Ditch That Textbook email newsletter. My blog, *Ditch That Textbook*, has an email newsletter where I share tools and ideas for using them every week. You can also get extra free resources with teaching ideas when you join. Sign up at DitchThatTextbook.com/101.

Use Twitter. My go-to source for teaching ideas is Twitter. As I have followed more and more educators who share great ideas, my Twitter feed has become like a custom-created newspaper, updated minute by minute, with new content. Want to get started on Twitter — or level up your Twitter game? Check out this free ebook, *A Beginner's Guide to Twitter for Educators*, at gclass. link/twitter.

Use other social media. Just because I love Twitter doesn't mean it's the only option! Pinterest offers tons of education-related boards and pins. Facebook has tons of educator groups, from general to very specific niches. Lots of educator creators use TikTok to share favorite tips, tricks, and ideas. Plus, Instagram has thriving communities of educators. Use what works for you!

Travel like a pro with Google Classroom

Google Classroom isn't the destination. It's the airport! Learn about the destinations where it can take you — both domestic (inside G Suite) and international (outside G Suite). Plan a trip that's a great learning experience you and your students will love. Google Classroom will make your teacher life easier, and you'll be able to fly all over the world with all the possibilities!

Check out the Google Teacher Podcast

Looking for Google ideas to use in your classroom? Want to keep up with the latest Google updates that affect your class? The Google Teacher Podcast is a show for educators that discusses all things Google in the classroom. To subscribe for free, search for it wherever you get podcasts or go to GoogleTeacherPodcast.com.

6

GIVE MEANINGFUL FEEDBACK

The late Grant Wiggins, author and education consultant, shared one of my favorite comments about the power of feedback on students in the classroom:

"Research shows that *less teaching* plus *more feedback* is the key to achieving *greater learning*. And there are numerous ways — through technology, peers, and other teachers — that students can get the feedback they need."

It's like a math equation. Less teaching plus more feedback equals greater learning.

I'm all for the "less teaching." But even if you don't like that part, we can certainly agree on the "more feedback" part. Feedback is crucial to student growth. It helps students know how good their skills are. Where they can improve. Where they're strong. It helps them see that they're growing and by how much.

Feedback is the teaching strategy with the highest impact in the *Teaching and Learning Toolkit* by the United Kingdom's Education Endowment Foundation. When done well, feedback can help students progress as much as 8 months faster than without quality feedback. Feedback is also low-cost compared to efforts like reducing class size, one-to-one tuition, and early years intervention, according to the Toolkit.

$$\text{Less teaching} + \text{More feedback} = \text{Greater learning}$$

Feedback is like the map app on your smartphone. You know what the destination is. You're given turn-by-turn instructions to help you get there. But if your battery dies and you stop getting feedback, it's easy to get lost. You lose valuable time, and your experience changes completely.

Types of comments in Google Classroom

Google Classroom is a feedback machine. Communicating with students is at the heart of almost every feature in Classroom. Feedback options in Google Classroom range from broad, whole-class comments to comments tied to an individual sentence, word, or even letter in a document or file. Here are several different ways to provide feedback in Google Classroom:

1. Announcements in the stream for everyone: These general comments can be used to inform students about class announcements and big-picture feedback for the entire class. By default, all students can see them. You can also add attachments to them, making them even more versatile.

2. Class comments in the stream for specific students: These comments can be given to small groups of students — even individual students. With the "All students" menu, you can pick and choose which students receive class comments. Create a class comment for a small group of students who need to finish work or who did exemplary work or who struggle with the same errors. When you post it, only you and those students will see the comment. Other students will not.

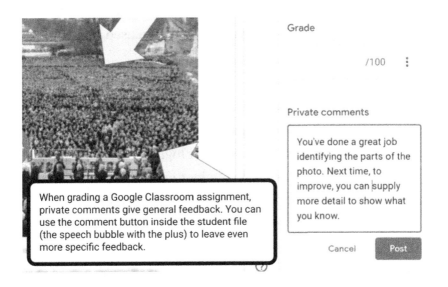

When grading a Google Classroom assignment, private comments give general feedback. You can use the comment button inside the student file (the speech bubble with the plus) to leave even more specific feedback.

3. Class comments inside an assignment: These comments are less general than class comments in the stream because they're tied to a specific assignment. Assignment class comments can be used for general class feedback. They can also be used for updates on the assignment and to answer questions about it.

4. Private comments inside an assignment: I think this may be the most powerful feedback tool in Google Classroom. Private comments are only visible to the student and the teacher. Inside a specific assignment, the teacher can message students about changes to make as well as strengths and weaknesses.

5. Document comments: Within many files that students turn in through Google Classroom, the teacher can add comments. The teacher can leave comments in those files by opening them in the assignment page or the Grades tab. Highlight a specific word or sentence, an image, a cell in a spreadsheet, or a shape on a presentation slide. Then click the **Comment** button (a speech bubble with a (+) inside). This is the most focused way to leave feedback for students.

6. Document annotations: Prefer to write or draw directly on student work? The Google Classroom mobile app lets you do that on a smart phone or tablet. Open student work as a PDF file. Use your finger or a stylus to draw, write or highlight. Do a two-finger pinch to zoom in and out. The student will be able to view and download your PDF file with your annotated comments.

7. Email from the People tab: If it's just easier to send feedback via email, Google Classroom can help. On the People tab, you can check which students you want to message. It loads a Gmail window where you can write your email. Select multiple students and it'll load an email with all of the students in the **bcc** field so they won't see who is receiving the message. This might be more effective if you have a longer message to share, something more permanent the student might want to keep, or if students are more likely to check their email.

Use other tools to leave Google Classroom comments

Google Classroom builds lots of ways to provide students with feedback right in the app. However, there are additional services that can help you leave feedback in different ways that can be a better fit for the assignment or more efficient. Leaving feedback connects with the airport analogy in the previous chapter. Sometimes, you want a domestic flight (something built in to Google Classroom). Other times, you take an international flight (something outside of Google Classroom that amplifies it).

Here are a few tools you can use in conjunction with Google Classroom. This list just scratches the surface of what's available!

Kaizena: Kaizena (kaizena.com) is a voice comment system that works inside Google Docs. Record comments with your voice or text. Students can respond the same way. (Free with paid upgrade)

Screencastify and Loom: These tools are screen recording tools. Screencastify (screencastify.com) and Loom (loom.com) can be used to record video narration of your feedback on student work. Start a screen recording with student work (a document, a slide presentation, etc.) on the screen. Use your voice to provide feedback. Use your mouse to point to or highlight parts you're talking about. When you're done, get a shareable link to the video and provide it to the student in a comment. The student can watch your recording, hear your voice, and see specific parts of their work you're addressing. (Free with paid upgrade)

Mote: Mote (justmote.me) lets you leave voice comments within your comments in Google Classroom, Docs, Slides, and

Sheets. It's a Google Chrome extension. Teachers and students can install it to leave voice comments to each other. (Free with paid upgrade)

Peer feedback: Fast feedback that's not from the teacher

We don't have to exhaust ourselves by providing endless amounts of feedback to students. Students can get helpful comments and suggestions from each other. Google Classroom can help us do all of this!

The peer feedback process can be set up in Google Classroom. Find steps on the next page. Before students start making comments on each other's work, it's helpful to have a framework for leaving effective peer feedback. Mark Gardner, a National Board Certified English teacher in Washington, wrote an article in Edutopia about the SPARK framework he uses to help his students reflect on each other's work. He said that many of his high school freshmen, for instance, aren't skilled enough to be effective editors, but they *can* reflect on each other's work. (More: gclass.link/spark and storiesfromschool.org.)

PEER EDITING
IN GOOGLE CLASSROOM

1. Create your assignment. Add a title and instructions. Specify points, due date and other details.

2. Create a document where students can share their work. You can name the file "Student links: Name of assignment" and use the same assignment name in your title. Attach the document to your assignment and choose **Students can edit file** from the drop-down menu.

3. Assign the assignment. Students work on their own files. When they finish, they click the **Share** button and create a shareable, **everyone can comment** link for their work. They copy the link and open the *student links document*. They write their name, highlight it, and add the link to their file.

4. Students open each other's work in the student links document. They add comments, reflecting on the work they just read.

5. In the end, each student re-opens their own work. They review the comments from other students and decide what revisions to make. Then, they submit their work in the Google Classroom assignment.

Mark encourages his students to meet these criteria:

Specific: Comments are linked to a discrete word, phrase, or sentence.

Prescriptive: Feedback offers a solution or strategy to improve the work.

Actionable: It leaves the peer knowing what steps to take for improvement.

Referenced: The feedback directly references the task criteria, requirements, or target skills.

Kind: All comments should be framed in a kind, supportive way.

This peer editing process helps students learn to evaluate each other's work and, in turn, learn about their own work and processes. They practice using criteria to reflect on others' work so that they'll be able to better reflect on their own work. In the end, each student gets feedback from multiple perspectives and not just the teacher's feedback. And the teacher isn't tasked with giving all the feedback!

Use the mobile app to be faster and more efficient

We saw earlier that the Google Classroom mobile app has features that the web browser version doesn't. When we know what the mobile app can do, we can use its unique features to add to what we do on our computers.

Voice typing is one of them. Many of us can type up to 30 or 40 words per minute. However, when you speak, that speed surges to 150 words per minute. This is part of the reason why tools mentioned earlier like Kaizena and Mote are popular. They put your feedback work into overdrive. Voice typing lets you share feedback, not with recorded audio but with readable text.

Leave comments and respond to messages in the Google Classroom mobile app. You probably have a voice typing feature on your mobile device. On my Android smartphone, it's a little microphone button when my keyboard pops up. Using voice typing (or dictation, as it's also called) is easy on a mobile device because it's already so seamlessly integrated into the device.

Pull up an assignment. Tap the text field to leave a comment. Then press that microphone button on your smartphone keyboard. Speak the comment and see how much faster it is than typing with your fingers or thumbs.

Push notifications in the Google Classroom app make this even faster. Many student actions can create one of those notifications that shows up at the top of your smartphone. (You can turn specific notifications on and off in the app's settings.) Pull that notification down with your finger and you may be able to reply within the notification. Type with your fingers — or use voice typing. You can have a response sent to the student in a matter of seconds. As you'll see below, best practices in feedback show that in most cases, the faster students get feedback, the better.

How to make the most of feedback in Google Classroom

Giving students feedback in the form of comments doesn't magically make learning better. Some feedback is better and more helpful than others. In fact, some feedback can even be detrimental. Here are some research-based suggestions for making your feedback as effective as possible:

Make feedback specific. General comments like "nice work" and "keep trying" don't help students learn what they need to improve. Feedback that specifies what the student can improve is better (Hattie and Timperley, 2007). In Google Classroom, this could mean adding comments to individual words and sentences in student attachments. It could also mean giving overall assignment comments that offer specific strategies for improvement.

Provide immediate feedback. When students get feedback sooner than later, it's usually better. One study showed that immediate feedback led to improved performance on assessments (Opitz, Ferdinand and Mecklinger, 2011). Another showed improved comprehension based on getting feedback right away (Samuels and Wu, 2003). In Google Classroom, the mobile app can help you respond quickly with voice-typed responses and push notifications. We'll also look at how to provide immediate feedback in assessments in a later chapter.

Provide feedback in three directions. Feedback can help students look at their work from multiple perspectives (Hattie and Timperley, 2007). These work when giving students feedback in Google Classroom in any way — individually through document comments, in a whole-class comment in the stream, or by any other means. Feedback can be categorized based on the purpose:

- First is to answer the question, "Where am I going?," referencing the student's goals for achievement, or *feed up.*
- Second is to answer the question, "How am I going?" This can be called *feed back.*
- Third is to answer the question, "Where to next?" This can be called *feed forward.*

Provide feedback at the four levels. Our feedback can often go further than whether an answer was right or wrong, whether an error was made or not. There are four levels at which feedback works (Hattie and Timperley, 2007). Again, these levels can help us leave varied, multi-faceted feedback.

- Task level: How well tasks are understood and performed. (Was the answer correct? Was it complete enough?)
- Process level: The main process needed to understand and perform tasks. (How did the student come to the result? Was that process effective?)
- Self-regulation level: Self-monitoring, directing, and regulating of actions. (Can you build confidence in the student? Can you help the student self-evaluate better?)

- Self level: Personal evaluations and affect (usually positive) about the learner. (How do you see the student as a learner and a person?)

Keep students growing with feedback in Google Classroom

Now you're leaving timely, specific, multi-faceted feedback in a variety of ways in Google Classroom. Look at you! Your students are moving forward, and you're saving some time by being efficient.

Let's stay on this roll. In the next chapter, we're going to look at the grading process. We'll identify how to make the most of the grading features in Google Classroom to save you time and keep the learning process moving.

Use these templates for class tomorrow

Don't do the work if you don't have to! I've created and collected dozens of "copy and assign" templates in Slides, Drawings, and Jamboard. Go to gclass. link/templates. Download or make a copy. Adjust as necessary. Assign to your students. Yep, that easy.

7

MAKE GRADING EASY

The assignments have been created. Students have done the work. Now, it's time to grade. Before you grade student work in Google Classroom, it's a good idea to remember what your grading philosophy is in the first place. Here are some questions to help you think through it:

- What role does grading play in the learning process for you?
- How important are overall grades? To you? To students?
- When you give points on assignments, what are you explicitly rewarding? What are you implicitly rewarding?
- Does your grading process show student proficiency? Mastery? How do you know?
- Are your grades based on percentage right/wrong? Are they based on your subjective judgment of students' work? What do those grades show about student proficiency?
- Do students know how you grade?

- Are grades really rewarding to your students? What is?
- Would students be more motivated by teacher comments and explanations than corrections and right/wrong markings? What's the right balance of those?
- How do you spend most of your time during grading? Is that a good use of your time?

Let's go back to Marie Kondo for a moment. Imagine your ideal lifestyle first. It's easier to build toward your goal when you know what your goal is. You can also strive toward a more intentional goal when you've thought it through carefully. If you have a clear idea of what you want your grades to accomplish, you can set up your policies and procedures — as well as your Google Classroom — accordingly.

The focus of this book has been about how to teach with Google Classroom, not just a tutorial on its features. I'll stick to that in this chapter, where I'll focus on ways to use Classroom to teach effectively. If you need some guidance on the basics of grading in Google Classroom, you can visit Google's support page here: gclass.link/grading.

It's easier to build toward your goal when you **know what your goal is.**

Here are six things you can do with Google Classroom to help achieve your goals in grading:

1. See everything with To Review

Getting a 30,000-foot flyover of your classes — or an individual class — can help. It can help you see how much grading you have so you can plan your time accordingly. It can help you see how your students are progressing as a class. It can also help you see which assignments — or types of assignments — may be challenging for your students.

Teaching takeaway: The To Review section organizes your grading. This section can be your organizational lifesaver. Find the To Review section under the three lines menu button in the top left corner. When you create an assignment, it's automatically added to the To Review section. You can display all classes at once or one class at a time. Move assignments from the To Review section to the Reviewed

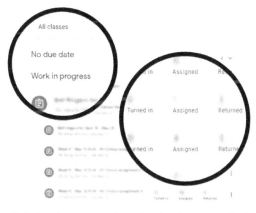

To Review gives you a grade overview, keeping you organized.

section and back with the three dots button on any assignment.

Imagine that your To Review and Reviewed sections are like two stacks of papers. To Review is the stack of papers to grade. Reviewed is the stack of papers you've finished grading. The To Review page is a way to keep organized without needing all that paper.

Save yourself clicks while entering grades

The way you enter grades in Google Classroom can impact how much time it takes. You do some actions repeatedly over and over in Google Classroom, like moving from textbox to textbox to enter information. Find a faster way and the time you save grows in multiples.

Teaching takeaway: Text expanders can save you time. Feel like you type the same thing over and over again when you grade? Text expander tools can save you lots of time. With these tools, when you want to type something you frequently type, you just type a short code instead. The text expander tool recognizes the short code and replaces it with the frequently typed phrase. You can even use a text expander to add links to helpful videos that explain ideas clearly for students in your comments.

An internet search for text expanders will help you find something that works for you. As of publication of this book, two good free options include AutoText (jitbit.com/autotext) and the Text Blaze extension for Google Chrome (blaze.today).

Teaching takeaway: Become friends with the tab button. Another trick involves the tab key. Pressing the tab key moves through each field one by one, left to right. Highlight the one you want. Type text or numbers when you get to the one you want. You can use the spacebar to click. Sometimes, using the tab key can be faster than using the mouse. Try different methods of entering data to find which is fastest for you.

Return assignments to students

The **Return** option is a versatile one. When you grade an assignment and provide feedback, it's standard practice to return an assignment to the student. But there are other times when you might want to use the **Return** feature.

For one, you might want to give back ownership rights for a file to a student. When a file is turned in to a teacher, the teacher temporarily is given those ownership rights. The student can't edit the file while it's turned in and can't see any comments or changes you make until you return it. You might return a file just so a student gets those ownership rights back.

Teaching takeaway: Integrate feedback throughout the learning process. Return an assignment to let students continue to work on it. When a student receives feedback after the assignment is done, there's nothing the student can do to improve. Some people call this "autopsy feedback." It's done postmortem, when the assignment isn't alive. If the assignment isn't live, many students don't see any benefit in reviewing that feedback. They've already moved their attention to the next assignment. It ends up being wasted time for the teacher and ineffective for student learning.

However, if you provide students feedback while the assignment is ongoing, the student has a reason to read it. It becomes useful. It helps the student to grow. Using the **Return** feature in Google Classroom facilitates that. Look over student work. Provide some suggestions and revisions. Then return it to revise and resubmit. It's a simple shift that can help students to progress based on your feedback.

Use rubrics when you grade

Rubrics can make your grading process more transparent. Set the criteria for grading before students start doing the work. Specify what it takes to reach each point level. That way, the expectations are clear. Google Classroom assignments make it easy to attach a rubric and give students information on how they'll be graded.

Provide feedback **throughout the learning process,** not just after grading. It's a **simple shift** that can help students progress.

Teaching takeaway: Use rubrics to reward results that you want. Teachers must be careful when grading with rubrics, though. A poorly crafted rubric can turn an activity into an exercise in checking all the boxes. Write 300 words? Check. Include 3 images? Check. Double space and 10-point font? Check. But what did the student write about? How did the student show understanding or mastery of a skill? It all goes back to identifying what you want to reward. Think about what you want the student to get out of the activity. How can you see it? How will you know the student learned? Write your rubric in such a way that the student is encouraged to pursue your goals, not just check off the boxes.

Teaching takeaway: The single-point rubric highlights how student work should be done. A novel way of grading with rubrics is to use the single-point rubric, a concept I learned about through a post on the *Cult of Pedagogy* blog. Read it at gclass.link/singlepoint. With

The Single-Point Rubric		
Where to improve	Criteria	Where you excel

traditional rubrics, teachers must create descriptions of student performance that don't meet the grading criteria. Why create descriptions of what we don't want students to do? The single-point rubric describes the top standard of performance, leaving room to describe where the student can improve and where the student exceeded standards.

A single-point rubric can be created in Google Classroom. Create a rubric with several types of grading criteria. Under each criterion is a single level of performance. Call it "proficient" or "meeting standards." Describe what is expected there. When grading with this rubric, click to give students the one point when meeting expectations. Don't click to give points when they don't. Use private comments and comments in the student's attached file to give feedback. Return the assignment to the student. If the student resubmits the work and achieves proficiency, give credit for it.

Use originality reports to check for plagiarism

Ever since Google Classroom was created, teachers have cried for a plagiarism checker. They've wanted help and a time-saving tactic for identifying what parts of student work were copied. Google responded with originality checks. Currently, as of the publication of this book, basic G Suite for Education districts can generate originality reports three times per class, while the paid premium G Suite for Education Enterprise districts can generate unlimited reports. (Check for updates to originality reports at gclass.link/updates.) The reports search publicly available websites for text that matches what the students have turned in. Check out a great explainer video by Jen Jonson at gclass.link/originality.

Teaching takeaway: Originality reports are only a tool in improving students' skills. These reports are a helpful tool for identifying which students' work wasn't their own. But they should only be that: a tool. They don't do the grading work on their own. Assessing student writing goes much further than deciding if a student plagiarized.

Assessing student writing goes much further than **deciding if a student plagiarized.**

It's up to the teacher to decide what happens if students' work isn't original. Should you punish the student in the gradebook, which affects the student's perceived level of proficiency? Or is there another route you can pursue to create change? Originality reports can also create teachable moments. Students can run originality reports on their own work before turning it in. Encourage them to run those reports. Then, talk to them about the results. These reports can create helpful one-on-one conversations with students to help them improve their researching and writing skills — skills that will serve them beyond their time in the classroom.

Email students with incomplete work

Keeping students on the ball with missing work is easy with Google Classroom. Click on an assignment in the Classwork tab, then click **View assignment**. Check the box next to a work status like **Assigned** to check all students who haven't completed the assignment. Then, click the email button at the top of the screen (the envelope next to the **Return** button). This will generate an email to just those students in that work status. This works for other statuses as well, like turned in, graded, and returned.

Teaching takeaway: Early, regular contact encourages students to complete work. Students forget assignments. Students fail to do assignments. Both are a reality of life. How will we follow up with them? Our actions impact whether they complete work and learn the lessons that come with it.

Your gradebook is under control!

You're becoming quite the grading guru. With the basics of grading in Google Classroom — and some important beliefs about how to make the most of grades — your grades are sending clear messages to students and encouraging them to grow.

An important part of grades is assessments. Assessments — including quizzes, tests and more — are a staple in most classes.

Google Classroom and various other tools can help. In the next chapter, we'll look at what good assessments look like with Google Classroom.

Want to send students a summary of all their assignments?

Go to the People tab and click a student's name. Then click the email icon (looks like an envelope) in the top right corner. Check the **Include student work summary** box. You can even add a personal message! If your district has guardian emails enabled, you can send these to guardians, too.

CREATE BETTER ASSESSMENTS

Have you ever used a Scantron machine? To use it, you would give students a Scantron sheet with the nefarious "make your mark heavy and dark" bubbles and a #2 pencil. Teachers would run those sheets through the Scantron machine, which would auto-grade those multiple-choice questions. There were fancier Scantron sheets with more than four answers per question so you could even do some limited matching in your questions.

Depending on the time of the year, the demand for the Scantron machine could get intense. At the end of the semester — final exam time — you might find yourself in line to use it. If somehow you jammed the machine and caused it to go out of commission, your colleagues' wrath would silently burn at you as they had to grade their tests (gasp!) by hand.

Since then, our digital devices and tools like Google Forms have made auto-grading available to anyone at any time — without getting in line for the Scantron machine. (Or using those little plastic templates you could lay over bubble sheets. Those were handy, too!)

Digital technology has democratized auto-grading. Now, when you talk about doing assessments in Google Classroom, many teachers' minds immediately go to Google Forms quizzes and tests.

But should they?

The case for and against auto-graded quizzes

There's a case to be made for auto-graded quizzes like those in Google Forms. Yes, people in certain education circles will cry, "We can do better than auto-graded multiple-choice quizzes! If you can Google the answer, ask a better question!" And that's true to some extent. But auto-graded quizzes do have a place. They can save us tons of time grading. They can give students lightning-quick feedback, which is a best practice for making feedback effective. Plus, these types of quizzes can give students the crucial repetitions that come from retrieving material from memory.

Auto-graded quizzes have their criticisms. Grant Wiggins listed seven keys to effective feedback in an *ASCD Educational Leadership* blog post: goal-referenced, tangible and transparent, actionable, user-friendly, timely, ongoing, and consistent (Wiggins, 2012). Some of those essentials — goal-referenced, transparent, user-friendly — get murky with auto-graded quizzes.

With auto-graded quizzes, it's hard to support the 4 C's: communication, collaboration, critical thinking, and creativity. They're limited. And let's not even get into the potential for cheating.

Can Google Forms quizzes be used effectively? I'd argue that they can — if you're using them in the right circumstances. In this chapter, we'll look at how to make a Google Forms assessment even better. Then, we'll look at ways to break away from the traditional quiz or test.

Note: If you need beginner help simply creating a Google Forms assessment, it's easy to find. Do a Google or YouTube search for "how to make a Google forms quiz." You'll find countless blog posts, tutorials and step-by-step videos. The rest of this chapter is focused on making the best assessments we can using Google Classroom and Google tools.

How to make Google Forms assessments better

There are all sorts of ways to assess students' understanding and skills. Assessment ranges from simple hands-up polls and verbal questions all the way to intricate portfolios of student learning. No matter what we're assessing, there are three key questions we should ask ourselves:

1. What do we want students to do?
2. How can we measure it?
3. Does this assessment truly and accurately measure what we're looking for?

If we want to use Google Forms to assess students, we must make sure that the Google Forms assessment will accurately measure what we want to measure. If we decide that a Google Forms assessment will work, here's how to build a better one.

1. Make a quiz from Forms, not Classroom

In Google Classroom's Classwork tab, you can use the **Create** button to make a new quiz assignment. Don't do that. Instead, go to Google Forms and create your assessment from there. There are a few reasons for this, writes Alice Keeler (2020):

> In a regular assignment click on "Create" and "Quiz Assignment." Easy peasy. It looks the same. It seems nice to have a couple of less clicks. **But "Quiz Assignment" does not just save you a few clicks.** It does funky things to your form in the background. You can't tell, but **some code is added to your form that gives you less control** over your form and how you reuse it. It's very annoying. And unnecessary.

Once you create your form, click the settings gear button and use the Quizzes tab to enable quiz features. Then, attach your form to an assignment in Google Classroom. If your Classroom is connected to your student information system (SIS) where you report grades, you can sync the quiz grades either way.

2. Use an "everything I wasn't asked" question

This strategy is a departure from traditional test practices, but it has great benefits. Add an extra paragraph-length text question at the end of a test. The prompt: "Everything I know about this topic but wasn't asked on the test."

On this question, students add details they remember, things they've learned, evidence of their mastery of the subject. It's a shift, letting students show us what they know instead of penalizing them for failing to know. One feels punitive. The other feels empowering.

These "everything I know" questions can be tricky to grade, though. Do we give a certain limited number of points for their answers there? Does it factor into the grade in other ways? Could a student demonstrate enough understanding in the "everything I know" question to override all other incorrect answers on the test? It seems to me like it should be an optional question. I think if I, the teacher, ask students the proper questions to demonstrate understanding, they should be able to answer those questions without having to add anything else to show full understanding — assuming they get all the questions right.

Here's an approach to grading it. Grade the test. Then, look at the student's response to the "everything I know" question. Then, ask yourself, "In light of what I see here and the standards, how should I adjust the student's grade to reflect his/her mastery?" This approach isn't fast, efficient or without faults. But then again, neither is a multiple-choice quiz or test. It is certainly more human. And it empowers students to show what they know.

Everything I know but wasn't asked on the test:

Your answer

It's a shift, letting students show us what they know instead of **penalizing** them for failing to know.

One feels **punitive.** The other feels **empowering.**

3. Let students create quiz and test questions

When we, the teachers, create quizzes and tests, students see them as something imposed on them by us. They don't understand the process. It's easy to call them unfair.

However, when they're part of the process, something changes. Students see what goes into making a fair, unbiased assessment. They start to see how hard "fair and unbiased" really is. They understand the reason for quizzes and tests and can help develop questions that reach that goal. Seeing the content through a test-maker's eyes makes them better test takers and they study better.

Ask students how they could show what they know on a quiz or test. Ask them to create a question or two that you can use on the test. Ask them what feels fair or unfair on quizzes or tests. Then, include their contributions as part of the quiz or test. The more we make them part of the process, the more they're bought in — and the less they feel an assessment is something done to them.

4. Choose how to release grades wisely

When setting up a form to be a quiz or test, you have a choice on how to release grades: immediately after each submission, or later, after manual review. Each option has benefits. Knowing the difference can help give students great feedback and preserve sanctity of the assessment.

Quiz options

Release grade:

(●) Immediately after each submission

( ) Later, after manual review
Turns on email collection

Option 1: Release immediately after each submission: This option will display a student's grade as soon as the assessment is complete. The student can click **View score** to see results right away. If you want them to refer to it later, send it via email later (if you're collecting email addresses) using the **Later, after manual review** option below.

When immediate release is helpful: If timely feedback is your top priority. If you have feedback written for correct and incorrect responses and loaded into your form, those will be displayed right away. To get the most benefit from that feedback, release it immediately. Students will still be in that mental state of wrestling with questions when they get immediate feedback. There won't be a time when it's more important to them than right after the quiz.

When immediate release isn't helpful: When the stakes are high and you want to be as certain as possible that students aren't sharing the answers. There's a balance here between taking steps to secure answers and giving the best feedback possible. A teacher could say, "I never want students to share the answers!" and might never choose this. However, when you hold the answers, in essence, you're diluting the power of your feedback. The longer you wait, the less impact your feedback will have. Sometimes, you must choose between the evils of students potentially sharing answers (which many students may never do) and less powerful feedback.

Option 2: Later, after manual review: This option will hold questions, answers, and feedback until later. Students won't be able to see them right away. This option lets you look back over questions with human eyes before sending grades to students. After you do, it's easy to release those grades and that feedback. In the form for your quiz or test, click the **Responses** tab and then choose **Individual.** Click the **Release score** button to choose to which students you'll send. Add a quick note if you'd like.

Pro tip: You can release scores more than once and to different groups. You can release scores in batches with different notes to different groups of students. Select certain students, type them a note, and send. Then, in another batch, select different students and send with a different note if you'd like.

When manual review is helpful: When students write out their answers. There's no easy way to auto-grade typed-out responses. Holding responses for manual review lets you read and respond. In the form, click **Responses.** You can grade individual student assessments by clicking **Individual** and advancing through each one. You can also grade by question, reading all responses to one question at a time. In either, you can assign a grade and give students individual feedback by clicking the pencil button. Manual review is also helpful when you want to give students general feedback about how the quiz went. You can look at the responses and results and send them informed feedback about their performance as a class through manual review.

When manual review isn't helpful: When you want to grade quickly. Manual review takes time. If you want to ask questions that the form can grade, let the form grade it for you! Quick feedback certainly has its advantages. It can be helpful to ask yourself, "On this assessment, should I ask longer questions that take longer for feedback, or should I ask shorter questions that can provide immediate feedback?" Sometimes, fast feedback makes a bigger long-term impact on students than longer feedback they have to wait for.

Google Forms can be a great feedback tool

It's easy to let Google Forms become a sterile, impersonal way to ask students questions and get grades in the gradebook. But it can be used with a focus on feedback. Plus, some adjustments such as those discussed above can really empower students to show what they know instead of playing "gotcha" with the facts they don't remember. Now, you're ready to use Google Forms to create quizzes and tests that go to the next level for student assessment!

Go beyond forms in Classroom assessments

Thankfully, when we use Google Classroom to manage our assignments, there's much more we can do to assess students digitally. Our quick formative assessments and our summative assessments at the end can go beyond the "answer these questions" mentality. If we want to see what students know — and what they can do with that knowledge — let's find some different ways for them to demonstrate. Let's look at some examples.

1. Create with content

The G Suite tools are fantastic content creation machines! They let students put their creativity on display and show us what they know. Today's workforce is looking not for what employees know, but what they can do with what they know. How can it be applied to serve the company, to serve others, to serve the world? That mindset can reap great rewards after students graduate.

Here are some of my favorite ways that students can create to demonstrate understanding with G Suite:

Infographics let students show what they know with a very brain-friendly verbal/visual mix. Use free icons with attribution from a source like *The Noun Project* (thenounproject.com) to spice them up. More: gclass.link/infographics.

Photo comic strips make students the stars of the activity. They can snap pictures with their webcams and add speech bubbles and thought bubbles for dialogue and reflection. More: gclass. link/comic.

Stop-motion animation can help students bring an idea in their minds to life. It uses Google Slides like a flip book. Students create animations and then flip through their slides. They can even record their animations with screen recording tools. More: gclass. link/animation.

Social media templates let students show what they know as if they were doing it on social media. These Google Slides templates feel like the social media and apps they love. But they're designed for academic work. Make a copy. Assign to your students. See what they create! More: gclass.link/social.

2. Record video

A great way for students to show you what they've learned is an idea educator Holly Clark shares: *press record*. Holly explains on her blog, *The Infused Classroom*, at hollyclark.org (2020):

> Technology provides an easy way to enable students to record or narrate the learning as it happens. **This makes their thinking and understanding visible.** Students explain their thinking process, expound as needed on that process, and share work by simply pressing record.
>
> This exercise is appropriate for all the steps of the learning journey. We do this so we as educators **can know more about our students as individual learners.**
>
> When we allow time for this, we really step up our digital pedagogy

game. It allows learners to see **growth over time** — and to begin to discover **individual strengths and weaknesses**. And it gives teachers the ability to see students as individuals with different **growth trajectories**, different **learning needs**, and different **perspectives**.

Armed with this understanding, we can better help **guide students toward their full potential**.

Read more about the "press record" idea in Holly's blog post at gclass.link/record.

Want to get started on this? Here are some great tools that work nicely with Google Classroom that let students record.

- **Flipgrid:** Students can easily respond to a question or prompt on Flipgrid (flipgrid. com). When they do, you can hear the intonation of their voices. You can see the expression on their faces. Especially when students record extemporaneously, you can watch as they process and explain the concept as a free flow from their mind. It's almost like being able to see their thinking.

- **Screencastify and Loom:** These screen-recording tools are helpful for anything that can be demonstrated on a screen. With Screencastify (screencastify.com) and Loom (loom.com), students narrate what they're doing as they do it. When you include a webcam video, you can even see their face as they explain. That's a lot of data you can use to assess their understanding.

- **Seesaw:** Seesaw (seesaw.me) is a learning platform with a great built-in screen recording tool. Seesaw's creative canvas lets students draw on the screen, pull in images and text, narrate their voice, and more. You can set up a Seesaw class for screen recording and manage the assignment in Google Classroom.

3. Use a graphic organizer

Guide students through their thinking and give them a space to work with graphic organizers. These activities provide much deeper learning than a traditional "drill and kill" worksheet. When done well, graphic organizers provide a structured space that walks students through a line of thinking. Students still have lots of autonomy to show what they know. When you provide the graphic organizers in Google Slides or Google Drawings, they're editable. Students get their own copy, can edit text, and in some cases, can move items around on the screen. (See Chapter 4 for more about "make a copy" attachments in Google Classroom.) For dozens of free, ready-made graphic organizers you can copy and assign to students, go to gclass.link/organizers.

Know what your students know

The more we know about what our students know and how they think, the better we can assess their learning. When we have more of that understanding, their grades are a better reflection of their progress in our class. We don't have to wonder, "Did those multiple-choice questions really show how much my students know?" We can be like learning detectives, gathering as many clues as we can to come to a solid conclusion.

Because Google Classroom is such a versatile tool, it can go beyond the basics. In the next chapter, you'll see how far Google Classroom can take you in lots of facets of your teacher life!

What is Google Drawings?

Google Drawings (drawings.google.com) is a graphic design tool that's part of G Suite. Think of Google Drawings like a digital posterboard. It's like Google Slides but just for one slide, without the slide management features of Slides. Drawings is great for images, infographics, and any kind of one-pager activities.

GO BEYOND THE BASICS

Google Classroom is what you make of it. A painter can make a canvas into a beautiful watercolor painting of trees, a funny caricature of a friend, or a stark, colorful piece of pop art. If you wanted to get into painting and wanted to emulate a favorite painter, you wouldn't look at the kind of brushes that painter bought. You'd probably look at the painter's style. The techniques. How the painter used the brush on the canvas.

If Google Classroom is the canvas, the possibilities for what you can create are equally open. Sure, you can create assignments, give feedback, and distribute grades. But why stop there?

In this chapter, you'll find lots of ways to go beyond the traditional classroom uses of Google Classroom. You'll see how far and wide you can use Google Classroom.

Using Classroom for extracurricular activities

If you host a club, a sports team, a school musical, or any other after-school activity, Google Classroom might become your best friend. Create a class in Google Classroom for your activity. Invite your student participants as students and encourage them to add the Google Classroom app to their smartphones. When you post announcements to your class, it pushes a notification to their phones. Interact back and forth with your participants in private comments and in announcement replies. Post files for them to access. Create Google Forms where they provide information. Here's the best part: If you use Classroom to communicate, you won't have to hand out your personal phone number, which can be fraught with all sorts of problems!

Have fun with students in Classroom

Your time spent in Google Classroom doesn't have to be all business all the time. Let's learn from hairstyles of the past on this one. (Or, in this case, sadly, hairstyles from the past that come back and just won't die!) Here's the mullet rule for Google Classroom: business up front, party in the back! Sure, we can take care of classwork in our assignments, announcements, questions, and quizzes. But that doesn't mean we can't have some fun! Create a topic in the Classwork tab for fun stuff. Or just add things to announcements in the Stream tab, like memes and silly pictures and videos. Compete in collaborative online games and post who the leaders are in Classroom. It's even more fun when students see themselves in the fun. Here are a couple of examples:

Digital escape rooms: Escape rooms have swept the world by storm. The concept: you and your friends visit one and are locked in a room. They're often themed with a back story, and you're swept into the story when you're locked in. Find clues that will help you to escape the room before time expires and you *win*! Digital escape rooms are a techy twist on these in online spaces. Students get a link to a website that's full of clues (whether they realize they're clues or not). Students use their problem-solving and deduction skills to unlock digital locks to escape. These can be layered with content from your class, too! Check out dozens of free pre-made escape rooms you can use and a guide to making your own at gclass.link/escape.

The 8 p*ARTS EduProtocol: This one is a learning activity, but it can be so much fun, your students might consider it a "just for fun" activity! 8 p*ARTs is an EduProtocol, a series of "lesson frames" created by educators Jon Corippo and Marlena Hebern. They're frames like a picture frame: the content inside changes, but the frame stays the same. In the 8 p*ARTS protocol, students describe a hilarious picture using all parts of speech. The photo changes, but the activity stays the same. It becomes a fun creative work where students try to upstage each other with funnier, more clever words and sentences. For more about the 8 p*ARTS protocol and other fun protocols, go to gclass.link/8parts.

Use satellite locations to expand Classroom

I've never been fancy enough to have a business card like this, but maybe you've seen one with the cities where a company has an office. It usually says something like "New York, Los Angeles, London, Tokyo." The funniest example of this I've seen was a t-shirt at the Covered Bridge Festival in tiny Parke County, Indiana, where I live. (Yes, we really have a Covered Bridge Festival. Our county prides itself as the covered bridge capital of the world!) A t-shirt at a stand there read: "Moscow. Paris. London. Bridgeton." Bridgeton, one of the little towns that celebrates the festival, is clearly *not* on the same level as the other three!

When a company lists these cities, usually the first city is home to the company's headquarters. The others are satellite locations where they have an office that does business but isn't the main hub.

Google Classroom can operate in this capacity, too. There's only so much you can do inside of Google Classroom itself. If you want to do more, chances are there's another G Suite tool (or a third-party app) that will help you. Call it your "satellite location." Like that big fancy business, you and your students do your work at your headquarters, Google Classroom. But sometimes, you step outside the headquarters and do work someplace else because that location has benefits the headquarters doesn't.

For example, a class Google Site can be a great satellite location. In Google Sites, you can embed videos from YouTube and Google Drive. It integrates with Docs, Slides, and Sheets seamlessly and can display those files for viewing right on a webpage. You can organize your site by page and make it easy to navigate. Can Google Classroom do all of this? No way! But Google Classroom is still the headquarters. All you must do is create the Google Site and link to it from Google Classroom. That way, all the great functionality and resources in the site are just a click away.

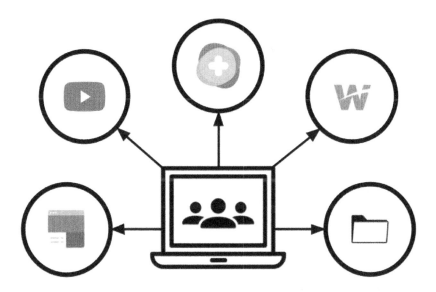

You can make satellite locations that can do more than Google Classroom with any number of apps.

- **A YouTube playlist** can make watching helpful videos easier.
- **A Wakelet collection** can gather images and links in one handy place.

- **A grid of videos on Flipgrid** can be a one-stop shop for student-created videos.
- **A shared folder in Google Drive** gives quick, easy student access to files.

If Google Classroom doesn't do it — or doesn't do it as well as we want — we don't have to throw up our hands and give up. Instead of lamenting, we can find a digital tool that *does* do what we want and link to it from inside Classroom.

Create a frequently asked questions (FAQ) document

As educators we field a *lot* of questions — from students and from parents. When is that permission slip due again? Can I turn that assignment in late? What does the atomic number mean

in the periodic table of elements? Answering the same questions repeatedly can be exhausting — especially when the questions make your inbox feel like a never-ending pile of emails.

By spending just a little time up front, you can make those questions feel a little less exhausting — and provide a 24/7 resource that can serve your students and their parents.

An FAQ page is a common part of many websites. In it, the website creator anticipates questions that the public will ask — or gathers questions they have actually asked. Then, the creator puts those questions on a page with answers to them. It's a living, breathing document where you can add more questions and answers as they arise.

You can make an FAQ page out of something as simple as a Google Doc you link to from Google Classroom. When students or parents ask a question, point them to the FAQ if the question has already been asked and answered. This can save you a ton of time and headaches. Plus, when they learn that the FAQ is there, they might find the answer there without asking you at all — the best solution for everyone!

Find ideas for creating great FAQ pages at gclass.link/faq.

Use Google Classroom outside of school

Google Classroom is available beyond schools. You can create and run a class in Google Classroom with a personal Gmail account. This means you can use many of the same features to communicate, post files, and create announcements for free without being connected to an educational institution. Some types of Google accounts (like education and nonprofit accounts) might not be able to connect to your personal Google Classroom, but personal Gmail accounts should work. The potential for this is limitless! Create a class in Google Classroom for a book club you host. Run church groups or committee meetings through Google Classroom. You could even organize a friends' night out with Google Classroom — as long as you and your friends don't think that's a little too nerdy!

Where will you use Google Classroom?

Now that you have a picture of how you can use Google Classroom inside and outside the classroom, it's time for action. What will you do with it? How will it change what you already do? What will it make possible that you didn't think was possible before? It's time to look forward.

10

WHAT'S NEXT?

Think back to the first chapter of this book. We looked at the war of one-star reviews that students all over the world waged against Google Classroom. Those students railed against Google Classroom. They claimed it was glitchy and broken, but if you look closely, you realize their concern went much deeper. Students were stressed. They were thrown out of their routines. It was hard to go forward as if nothing had happened.

I wonder how things might have been different if their teachers understood all they could have done through Google Classroom to provide for their students. Instead, they might have . . .

- Checked in with students through a simple "how are you?" Google Form
- Created "good morning" videos in Flipgrid, posting them to Classroom to give students a warm, familiar face
- Brought a little joy and levity to an otherwise frustrating and sad time by connecting to students' interests

In short, they might have used Classroom to be part of the solution instead of adding to the problem.

How can we improve our practice so this doesn't happen to us in the future? Progress can come in various forms.

Get new ideas

People are constantly sharing ideas on making the most of Google Classroom and Google tools in schools. You'll find them in blogs and websites. On social media. In podcasts and YouTube videos. I think all these sources are like a mountain stream. You come across the stream on a hike and never realized it was there. Now that you know it's there, you can come back whenever you'd like. The water never stops flowing, so you can go back every once in a while or every day. It doesn't matter to the stream. While you're there, you can dip your toe in the waters or jump in water above your head. You can fish and kayak and skip rocks. You can use it for whatever you need.

When you find resources that fuel you as an educator, you can always turn back to them. Sometimes, all the resources can overwhelm you. There are so many, and there will be even more tomorrow. Just because the resources keep flowing doesn't mean you have to touch every molecule in the proverbial waters. Use those resources as much or as little as needed — and however they best suit you.

I love freely sharing ideas to use in the classroom. Here are some of my best resources:

The companion site for this book: I've shared lots of resources at <u>GoogleClassroomBook.com</u> that you've seen in this book plus more. This site is available for anyone for free, so feel free to share.

The *Ditch That Textbook* email newsletter: In this weekly email, I share practical teaching ideas you can use right away. Think of it as a pipeline of new ideas landing directly in your inbox. When you subscribe, you'll also get three free ebooks, including one called *101 Ways to Ditch That Textbook with G Suite*. To subscribe, go to gclass.link/email.

The Google Teacher Podcast: In this podcast, co-host Kasey Bell and I share Google news and updates, ideas to use in the classroom, interviews with educators, questions from listeners, and resources to check out. To subscribe and listen, go to GoogleTeacherPodcast.com.

More Google ideas: You can find the best articles, videos, tutorials and resources on Google tools I've created on my Google Ideas page at gclass.link/ideas.

Google Slides ideas: My absolute favorite G Suite tool is Google Slides. You can make so much more than slides for oral reports. It's the best creation tool in G Suite. Get lots of ideas to use in class at gclass.link/slides.

Twitter has been a rich source of ideas for me, too. I can always find new ideas, updates on Google tools, and inspiration there. If you start by looking at some great hashtags, you can find ideas to use in class, people to follow, and articles to read. It's also the starting point for communication and connection with fellow educators. I suggest these hashtags: #GoogleEDU, #GSuiteEDU, #edtech, and #ditchbook, the hashtag connected to my book, *Ditch That Textbook*.

Reflect on your practice

We educators are a busy sort. We're constantly teaching. Grading. Emailing. Meeting. Trying to squeeze bathroom breaks in the middle of everything. We spend our after-school hours coaching, sponsoring clubs and activities, going to our students' performances. Some things end up taking a backseat to all those busy activities. Sometimes, those things are important things.

For me, one of those things has always been reflecting on my practice. I struggle to stop and reflect. I have always seemed to plan lessons, teach, and then mindlessly move on to the next thing.

John Dewey is attributed with one of my favorite maxims on reflective practice. Although I can't find where (or if) he wrote these words, the idea echoes in so much of his work: "We do not learn from experience. We learn from reflecting on experience." This goes for students, but it certainly goes for us as educators. We often get so busy that we don't stop to learn from our experiences.

One of my favorite practices is to take a moment and reflect on how lessons went throughout the day. Jot those reflections next to your lesson plans. Ask yourself questions like, "What went well? What can I improve? What do I try next? What do I try next year?" I've always used paper lesson plan books, so for me, the next step is logged there, but you could use anyplace that makes sense. Hang on to those lesson plans as an artifact of your growth and a reference for future teaching.

Share your ideas

Early in my teaching career, I benefitted from so many educators who shared their ideas and resources online. At some point, I realized something. If they were the only ones who created, the internet — and the educator resources there — would be a shell of what it could be. I realized it's up to me to share, too. That means it's up to you, too.

So, how can you share?

Share on social media. Find your social platform of choice. Twitter has always worked for me, but educators also flock to Instagram, Pinterest, Facebook, TikTok and Snapchat. Tinker with the best way to reach others. Don't worry if your following is small. The gold is in the reflection and how you internalize and synthesize your practice when you share. Also, when you share on many of these platforms, you're sharing something that people may find in the future when they connect with you. Share good stuff for those people when they eventually find you.

Share with colleagues. The people around you are the ones on whom you might have the most influence. It's powerful when you see something that works shared by someone you know. You're more likely to try it when it's not shared by a nameless face from the internet. Plus, when you share good stuff with your colleagues, you're building up the school and district where you work. That benefits your students and the community where they live.

Share at conferences. Yes, you read that right. Teacher conferences are magical places. Ever since I was a new teacher, I've always marveled at the electric atmosphere of conferences where teachers share their craft, their successes, and their failures with others. You'll find them in physical venues where teachers meet face to face. You'll also find them online. (For years, I've hosted the free Ditch That Textbook Digital Summit in December. You can get details and register at DitchSummit. com.) It's easy to dismiss this idea by saying, "What do I have to offer? I'm not accomplished enough to present at a conference." The truth is that everyone has an experience and a perspective to share. When you keep it to yourself, you rob others of that experience and perspective that could be so valuable to them. Plus, you don't have to be a public speaking expert or a fabulous graphic designer with impeccable slides. Just share. You know how we are as educators. We look for the heart of those we're connecting with. We do it with students all the time. We're just the same with fellow educators. We'll see your sharing heart and thank you for it. Plus, we're all in this to get better for the sake of our students. If you can help others do that, they'll be grateful you were brave enough to share.

Try new things

As you learn new features about Google Classroom and see possibilities for your practice, you might start thinking about what you might change. "Nah," you might convince yourself. "What I'm doing is OK. What if I tried that new idea and failed?"

Brace yourself. I'm about to share one of my favorite ideas from the keynote speeches I give to teachers!

Many times, we won't try new ideas because of that fear of failure. We think new ideas are too risky, so we stick with what we've always done because it feels safe. I can understand this belief. But I think it's rooted in an incorrect definition of the word *risky*. I think it's time that we reframe the word *risky*.

To do that, let's start with what feels safe to us. For me, giving direct instruction in front of the classroom has always felt safe. It has always made me feel comfortable. Teachers have done it for ages. It must be safe. But many times, my direct instruction gets boring and it's ineffective. What feels safe to me is actually risky because it doesn't engage my students. When they quit paying attention, they might as well be somewhere else. In that case, what I thought was safe teaching turned out to be risky teaching.

So, if safe teaching can be risky teaching, is the inverse true? Can risky teaching be safe? Think of a new idea you want to try. It has lots of potential, but you're not sure how it'll go. If you try it and it doesn't go well, it's not a failure. You can reflect on it, giving you more data on how to do it better next time. If it does go well, though, you may have a great new lesson that connects with your students and is effective. You can't go wrong here! Either way, your teaching that feels risky is safe.

Taking some risks may be one of the safest things we can do. Many times, the thing we fear most is just a mirage of what could happen, something that likely will never happen at all.

You can do this!

A teacher's impact is far-reaching. There's no way of knowing how much you've affected your students' lives and their futures. It's like a pebble thrown in the middle of a still pond. The ripples start small and close together. But with time, their reach extends to the very limits of the pond and beyond. The longer you teach, the bigger your ripple effect will be on the world.

Google Classroom isn't going to cause those positive ripples in the pond of life. As we've seen throughout this book, it's just a tool. But with the right tools in hand, we can build something impressive, something that will survive long after us. Google Classroom isn't the surrogate of a great teacher. It's the tool in the hands of a great inspirational, pedagogical craftsman (or craftswoman).

Start your best teaching with your mind and your heart. Be brave enough to bring those dreams into reality. Use the tools you need most to craft the education your students need. This is how we change the world as educators, and I'm excited for the impact you'll have on your students.

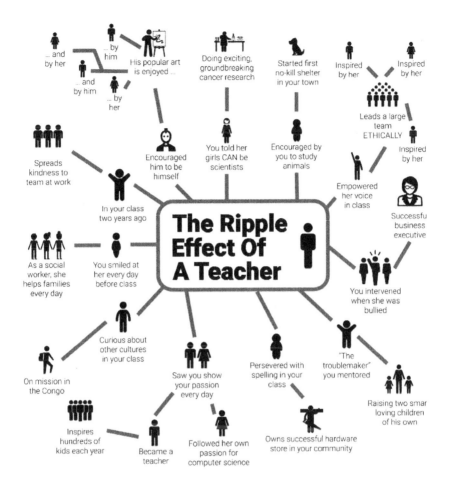

The Ripple Effect Of A Teacher

... and by her

... by him

... and by him

... by her

His popular art is enjoyed ...

Doing exciting, groundbreaking cancer research

Started first no-kill shelter in your town

Inspired by her

Inspired by her

Leads a large team ETHICALLY

Inspired by her

Spreads kindness to team at work

Encouraged him to be himself

You told her girls CAN be scientists

Encouraged by you to study animals

Empowered her voice in class

Successful business executive

In your class two years ago

As a social worker, she helps families every day

You smiled at her every day before class

You intervened when she was bullied

Curious about other cultures in your class

On mission in the Congo

Saw you show your passion every day

Persevered with spelling in your class

"The troublemaker" you mentored

Raising two smart loving children of his own

Inspires hundreds of kids each year

Became a teacher

Followed her own passion for computer science

Owns successful hardware store in your community

NEVER forget your **impact.**

ABOUT THE AUTHOR

Matt Miller taught in public schools for more than 10 years, teaching all levels of high school Spanish. In his career, he planned nearly 12,000 class lessons. He taught more than half a million instructional minutes. And he graded work for nearly 2,000 days of class. He was recognized for classroom excellence with the WTHI-TV Golden Apple Award and as a two-time nominee for the Bammy! Awards Secondary Teacher of the Year.

He's the author of five books: *Ditch That Textbook, Ditch That Homework, Don't Ditch That Tech, Tech Like a PIRATE,* and *Do More with Google Classroom.* He is a Google Certified Innovator and the co-host of the Google Teacher podcast, a show for educators with more than 1 million downloads. He holds a Master of Education in curriculum and instruction from Indiana State University.

He lives in west central Indiana and says that he's living the dream: happily married with three kids, three dogs and a massive cell phone bill.

Bring Matt To Your School, District Or Event

Workshops: When you invite Matt to present at your school, district, or event, you'll see results. Teachers use his practical ideas in the classroom the next day. His workshops and conference breakout sessions are hands-on. Teachers learn new ideas for the classroom and practice them firsthand so they're ready to implement. They come away infused with pedagogy, brain science, and inspiration, going far beyond the passive, "check out this cool website" style of professional development.

This was a day you walk away excited and trying to figure out **what you're going to try first**!

— Workshop participant via Twitter

Matt is **always a hit** at CUE events. His skills, passion and humor resonate. Behind the scenes, Matt's **a true professional**: on time, flexible, and a joy to work with.

— Jon Corippo,
former Chief Academic Officer, CUE Inc.

Keynote speeches: After Matt's keynote speeches, educators see their mission in education differently and are ready to claim it. He tells his own story of ditching his textbooks — including the struggles and doubt. He uses the whole stage, performing his speech with props, costume, and acting techniques. He encourages teachers to take risks, grow through their experiences, and create the classroom of their dreams. Just as important, he helps them see how vital they are and how much the world depends on them.

For more information about Matt's presentations and speeches, send an email to **hello@ditchthattextbook.com**.

REFERENCES

Clark, H. (2020, September 17). Rethinking Digital Assessment. Retrieved November 06, 2020, from https://www.hollyclark. org/2020/06/15/press-record-making-thinking-visible-in-the-classroom/

Gonzalez, J. (2020, February 23). Meet the Single Point Rubric. Retrieved November 06, 2020, from https://www. cultofpedagogy.com/single-point-rubric/

Hattie, J., & Timperley, H. (2007). The power of feedback. Review of educational research, 77(1), 81-112.

Keeler, A. (2020, November 04). Google Classroom: Do NOT Use Quiz Assignment. Retrieved November 06, 2020, from https://alicekeeler.com/2020/07/26/google-classroom-do-not-use-quiz-assignment/

KonMarie Media, Inc. (2020, July 27). Rule 2: Imagine Your Ideal Lifestyle — KonMari: The Official Website of Marie Kondo. Retrieved November 09, 2020, from https://konmari.com/marie-kondo-imagine-your-ideal-lifestyle/

Opitz, B., Ferdinand, N. K., & Mecklinger, A. (2011). Timing matters: the impact of immediate and delayed feedback on artificial language learning. Frontiers in human neuroscience, 5, 8.

Samuels, S. J., & Wu, Y. (2003). The effects of immediate feedback on reading achievement. Unpublished manuscript, University of Minnesota, Minneapolis. Available online from http://www.tc.umn.edu/~samue001/webpdf/immediate_feedback.pdf

Wiggins, G. (2012, September). Seven Keys to Effective Feedback. Retrieved November 06, 2020, from http://www.ascd.org/publications/educational-leadership/sept12/vol70/num01/Seven-Keys-to-Effective-Feedback.aspx

Made in the USA
Middletown, DE
04 January 2021